by Chris Kringel

A Complete Guide to the Basics

Contents

Tuning Your Bass	2
Lesson 1—First and Second Position	3
Lesson 2—Movable Scale Forms	6
Lesson 3—Fifth Position	10
Lesson 4—Intervals	15
Lesson 5—Key Review	20
Lesson 6—Chord Theory	25
Lesson 7—The Dominant Scale	32
Lesson 8—Slap Bass	35
Lesson 9—Locking In	40
Lesson 10—Putting It All Together	43
Review	48

Track 1

Introduction

Welcome to Level 2 of *Play Bass Today!*, the series designed to prepare you for any style of bass playing. Whatever your taste in music—rock, blues, jazz, country—*Play Bass Today!* will give you the start you need.

In Level 1, we covered the basics of music and of the bass. In Level 2, we'll really expand on that knowledge. We'll learn new scales, grooves, and playing techniques. We'll even learn how to play higher up on the bass neck. We'll explore a variety of essential tools that will prepare you for any style of bass playing. As always, you'll be accompanied by a band on most songs, making learning to play bass enjoyable and easy.

Recording credits:

Todd Greene, Producer
Jake Johnson, Engineer
Doug Boduch, Guitar
Scott Schroedl, Drums

Chris Kringel, Bass
Warren Wiegratz, Keyboards
Michael Landers, Narration

ISBN 978-0-634-02848-9

7777 W. BLUEMOUND RD. P.O. BOX 13819 MILWAUKEE, WI 53213

Visit Hal Leonard online at
www.halleonard.com

Tuning Your Bass

The bass's four open strings should be tuned to the pitches E–A–D–G (low to high). These can be found on track 2 of the accompanying audio, or from one of the following sources:

The Piano

If you have a piano or keyboard, play each note shown one at a time, and tune each bass string to match its corresponding pitch.

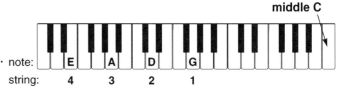

middle C

note: E | A | D | G

string: 4   3   2   1

A Pitch Pipe

A pitch pipe, available from most music stores, may also be used to find these pitches.

An Electronic Tuner

An electronic tuner will "listen" to the sound of each string as you play it and indicate whether the pitch is too high or too low. You should adjust each string accordingly.

Relative Tuning

The following procedure is called *relative tuning* because the strings are tuned relative to one another. It's a great way to tune your bass when no pitch sources are available.

1. Tune the 4th string E to a piano, a pitch pipe, an electronic tuner, or the audio. If none of these are available, approximate E the best you can.

2. Press the 4th string at the 5th fret. This is A. Tune the open 3rd string to this pitch.

3. Press the 3rd string at the 5th fret. This is D. Tune the open 2nd string to this pitch.

4. Press the 2nd string at the 5th fret. This is G. Tune the open 1st string to this pitch.

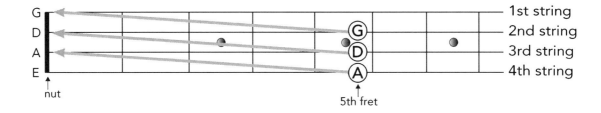

First and Second Position

Track 3

Let's take some time to review the notes we learned in Level 1. *First position* is the area of the bass neck from the open strings to fret 4. *Second position* is the area from the second to the fifth fret.

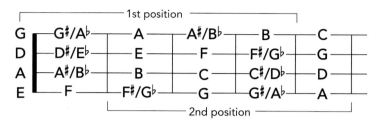

Remember: Notes like F♯ and G♭ are called *enharmonic equivalents*—two different note names for the same pitch. Either spelling is acceptable. There is no difference in the way these two notes are played or in the way they sound.

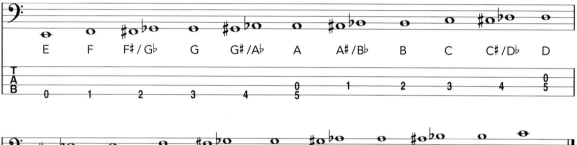

When playing in a position, we generally follow the *one-finger-per-fret-rule*—first finger on the first fret, second finger on the second fret, third finger on the third fret, and fourth finger on the fourth fret. That describes the first position. If you need to reach the fifth fret, move your hand to second position—with your first finger on the second fret and your pinky on the fifth fret.

first position

second position

Let's try some bass lines using the notes in first and second position.

Track 4

Position One

Position Two

Track 5

Reminder: If you see a dot (•) above or below a note, it means to play the note short, or *staccato*. To do this, release pressure on the fret—or if it's an open string, touch it lightly—with your left-hand finger.

Stuck At Zero

Track 6

► Practice this slowly to make sure each note is staccato.

By the way, if you're plucking the strings with your fingers, be sure to alternate consistently back and forth between your index and middle finger. If you're playing with a pick, use either all downstrokes or alternate picking (downstrokes and upstrokes).

Metronome

A *metronome* is a device used to mark time. Practicing with a metronome forces us to listen to a consistent beat (or click) and match it. The tempo, or rate, of the click is measured in *bpm's*—beats per minute. Metronome practice improves consistency, listening, and matching skills.

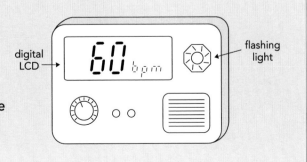

digital LCD

flashing light

Practicing with a Metronome

Let's try practicing with a metronome. We'll place the metronome click on different beats within the same example.

Metronome on beats 1, 2, 3, and 4.

Metronome on beats 1 and 3.

Metronome on beats 2 and 4.

► This one's a little tricky, so take it slowly.

Now we'll play along with the whole band to a *click track*—which is basically a metronome used when recording a band. The click track will be on beats 1, 2, 3, and 4.

Seesaw

The click track will be on beats 1 and 3.

Boots

► Count beats 2 and 4 silently.

Movable Scale Forms

Track 10

In Level 1, we talked about major and minor scales, and how we can use them to play in keys. We also discovered that some scale shapes are movable. Just find the desired root note (on strings 3 or 4) then apply the pattern of your choice—and there's your scale!

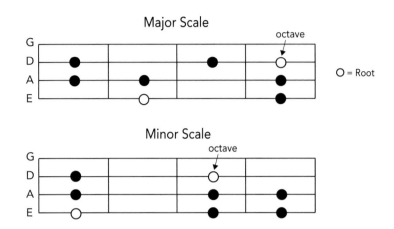

Let's try moving these scale forms around a bit so you can see how they work. First, we'll use the major shape—play a C major scale, then move down a half step to play a B major scale. Then we'll try the minor shape—play an F# minor scale followed by Bb minor.

Track 11

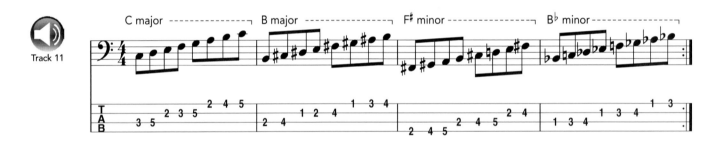

You've just played four scales using only two shapes! The beauty of these shapes is that you don't have to think of them only in block form. Let's look deeper and break them down by string.

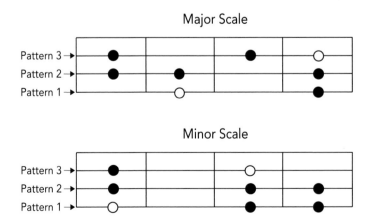

Scales on a Single String

Let's try a G major scale *on one string*—using the patterns we just broke down. Here's how we do it: Play the first string pattern, then skip one fret (one whole step); then play the second string pattern, skip one fret (one whole step); then play the third string pattern. We'll be moving up the neck into some uncharted territory, so pay close attention.

G Major

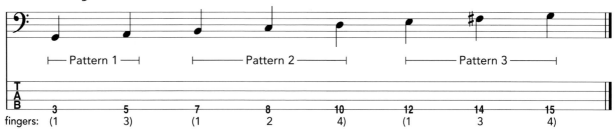

Now we'll try this same approach with the G minor scale.

G Minor

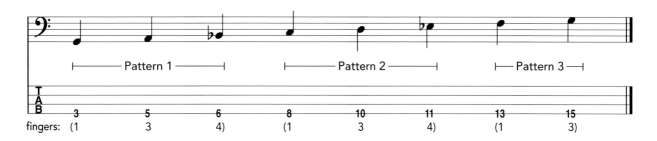

Now, let's try a C major scale on one string. Keep the same fingers playing the same notes as you do when you play the scale normally; except for the first string pattern—use your first and third fingers (see below).

C Major

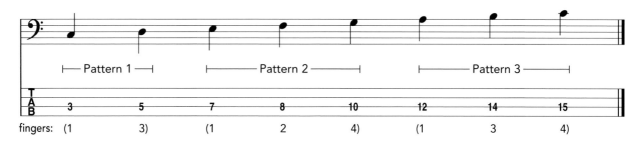

Now try C minor.

C Minor

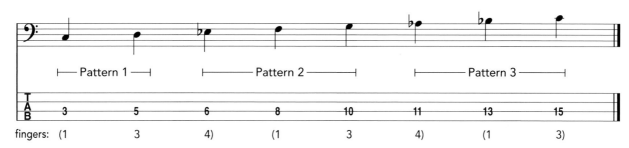

Now we'll play some songs moving up and down the neck using these patterns, so you can see their practical use. Again we'll be moving up the neck of the bass—to notes and positions you might not be familiar with—so pay close attention to the tablature. This is a great way to learn those notes! This song uses octaves up high on the neck.

Bee C's

Track 13

► Pay close attention to notes and shapes on the A string.

Octaver

Track 14

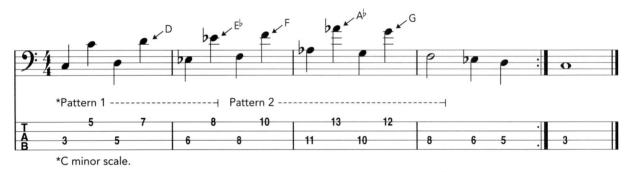

Sixteenth Notes and Rests

Sixteenth notes look like eighth notes, but they have two flags or beams:

Sixteenth rests also have two flags:

Two sixteenths equal one eighth. Four sixteenths equal one quarter. Here's a diagram showing the relationship of sixteenth notes to all the rhythmic values you've learned:

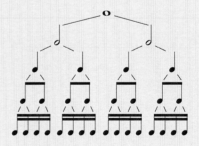

To help you keep track of the beat, consecutive sixteenth notes are connected with a beam. To count sixteenths, divide the beat into four, and count "1-e-&-a, 2-e-&-a, 3-e-&-a, 4-e-&-a":

1 e & a 2 e & a 3 e & a 4 e & a

Because sixteenth notes move so quickly, you'll find them easier to play if you alternate between your index and middle finger when plucking the strings. If you use a pick, try alternating downstrokes (⊓) with upstrokes (∨).

Track 15

Alternate Sixteenths

Track 16

Punk Sixteenths

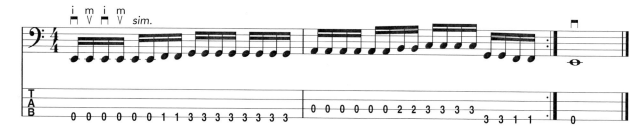

Now try some sixteenth rests; this gets a little tricky, so go slow—and don't forget to count. (The first time through this, concentrate on counting; the second time, watch what your right hand is doing, and compare it to what's shown.)

Track 17

Rest Up

Track 18

Brake Fluid

Fifth Position

Track 19

So far, we've learned to read in the first and second position of the bass, and we've explored up the neck using movable scale forms—skills that will serve us well in many situations. Now let's expand our horizons by learning to read in a new area: the *fifth position*.

■ Fifth position starts on high C at the 5th fret—this time played with the index finger.

Starting at the 5th fret allows us to access several more notes on the G string that weren't available to us in the first and second position. Of course, it also gives new fingerings for many familiar notes. Playing in this position can help us create smoother, more consistent bass lines.

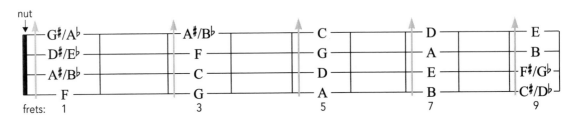

You may notice that, since we no longer have the open strings working for us, we sometimes have to cover more frets—in general, follow the one-finger-per-fret rule, but allow your pinky to cover both the 8th and 9th frets.

Track 20

▶ Say the notes aloud as you play them.

Fifth Position

To get a better feel for this position, try a few scales and songs. This first scale can be played in first position or fifth, so try it both ways.

Track 21

A Minor

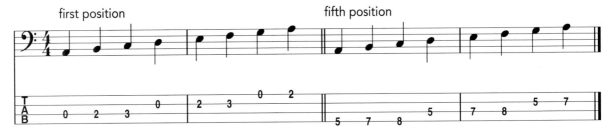

Rhythmic

► Make sure to alternate fingers when plucking with the right hand.

Now try this E♭ major scale.

E♭ Major

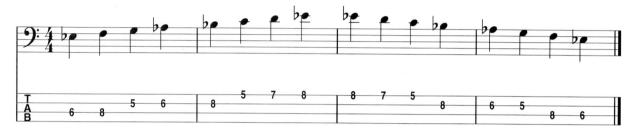

Mother Earth

Combining Sixteenths with Eighths

Now we're going to start combining sixteenth notes and eighth notes over the same beat. This can get a bit confusing, so take it slow and don't forget to count.

Eighth & Two Sixteenths

count: 1 e & a 2 e & a 3 e & a 4 e & a   1 (e) & a 2 (e) & a 3 (e) & a 4 (e) & a

1 & 2 & 3 & 4 &   1 (e) & a 2 (e) & a 3 (e) & a 4 (e) & a   1 (2 3 4)

Two Sixteenths & an Eighth

Sixteenth, Eighth, Sixteenth

Remember: A *dot* adds half the value to a note. So, in this case, a dotted eighth note equals three sixteenth notes, or an eighth plus a sixteenth.

Dotted Eighth & Sixteenth

► Take this one slowly and be sure to count.

12

Sixteenth & Dotted Eighth

Track 29

count: 1 e & a 2 e & a 3 e & a 4 e & a   1 e (& a) 2 e (& a) 3 e (& a) 4 e (& a)

1 & 2 & 3 & 4 &   1 e (& a) 2 e (& a) 3 e (& a) 4 e (& a)

This song uses more than one position.

Funky Feel

Track 30

► Shift your left hand when moving to a new position.

Sometimes, you'll use more than one position to play a song. For instance, you might start in open position, then move up to fifth position for some higher notes, and then move back down again. If there's no tablature, survey the song before playing it to determine what positions to use.

Switch Position

Track 31

Memorizing Notes

Learning the location of all the notes on your bass is essential. Here's a good way to practice memorizing them. We'll start by naming the notes vertically on the first fret: F–A♯/B♭–D♯/E♭–G♯/A♭. Then the third fret: G–C–F–A♯/B♭. Now continue up the neck naming notes on the fifth, seventh, and ninth frets. This is a fast way to learn all your notes. Every time you pick up your bass, do this exercise; you'll be surprised at how fast you'll know your bass neck.

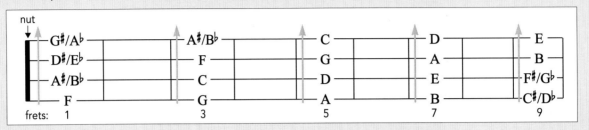

When you conquer the first, third, fifth, seventh, and ninth frets, move on to the second, fourth, sixth, and eighth frets. They should be easy because you'll already know the notes next to them!

When you know fifth position well enough, try some new songs, like these!

Track 32

Upside Your Head

► Be warned: there are some pinky stretches here!

Track 33

Tongue in Cheek

14

Track 34

Lesson 4 | Intervals

An *interval* is the term for the distance between two notes. In Level 1, we looked at the intervals of a half step (one fret) and a whole step (two frets). Now we'll look at intervals in relation to scales and chords. Every interval has two parts to its name:

- **number**—second, third, fourth, fifth, sixth, etc.
- **quality**—major, minor, perfect, diminished, or augmented

Knowledge of intervals is essential to building great bass lines. For the next twelve examples, we'll play an interval, and then a song based around that interval—so you can hear what it sounds like. All examples will be in the key of C.

Minor Second

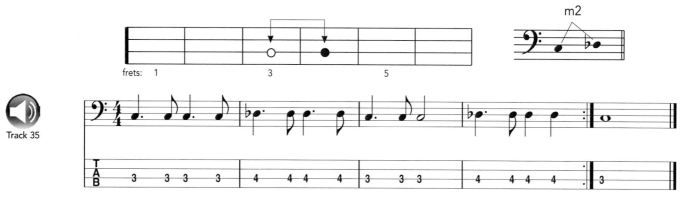

Track 35

Major Second

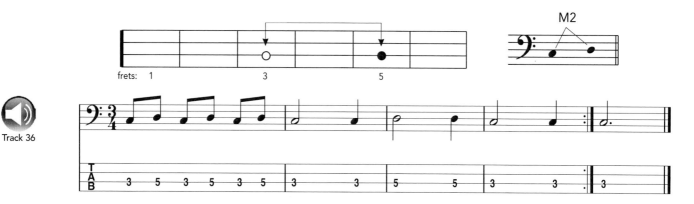

Track 36

Minor Third

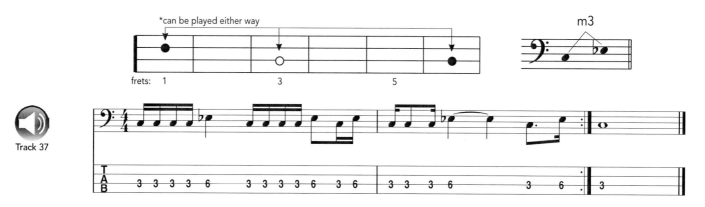

Track 37

Major Third

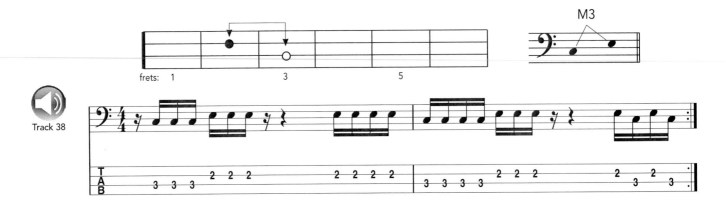

Track 38

Perfect Fourth

A *fourth* is called "perfect" because it remains the same distance from the tonic whether it's found within a major or a minor scale.

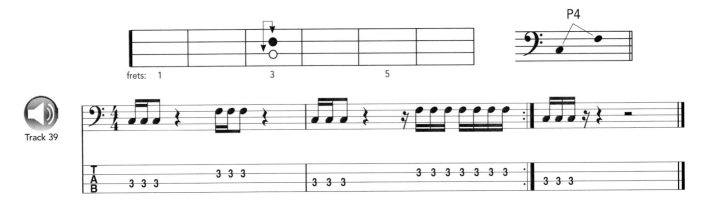

Track 39

Augmented Fourth or Diminished Fifth

Augmented means to "raise one half step"; diminished means to "lower one half step."

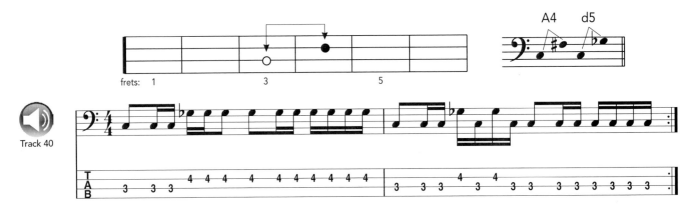

Track 40

Perfect Fifth

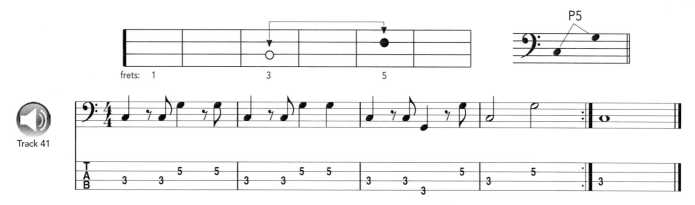

Track 41

Augmented Fifth or Minor Sixth

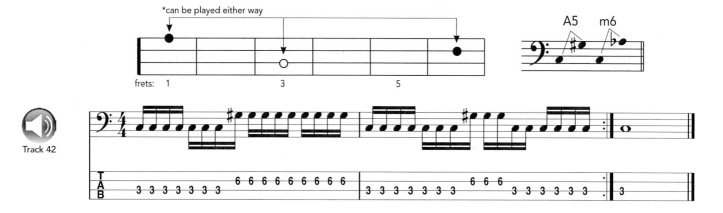

Track 42

Major Sixth

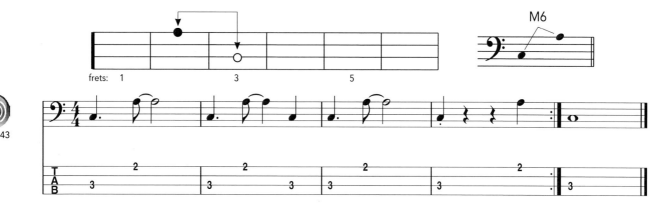

Track 43

Minor Seventh

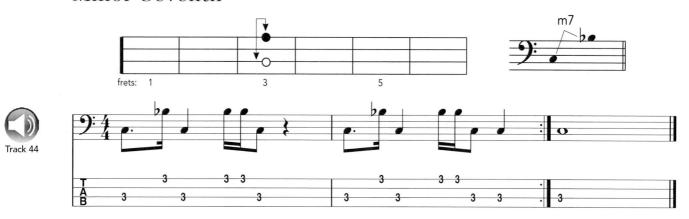

Track 44

Major Seventh

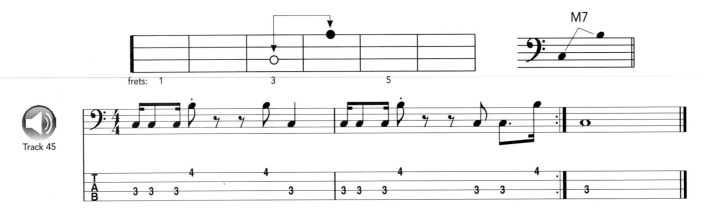

Track 45

Octave

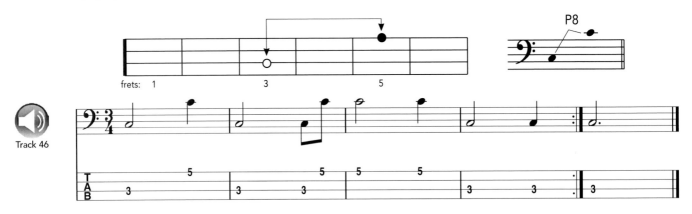

Track 46

The Shuffle Feel

The *shuffle feel* is a very common element of rock, blues, pop, and jazz music. It uses a new rhythmic value called a "triplet."

By now, you know that a quarter note divided into two equal parts is two eighth notes. And a quarter note divided into four equal parts is four sixteenth notes. But a quarter note divided into three equal parts? This is an *eighth-note triplet*:

Triplets are beamed together with a number 3. To count a triplet, simply say the word "tri-pl-et" during one beat. Tap your foot to the beat, and count out loud:

Shuffle rhythm can be derived from a triplet rhythm by inserting a rest in the middle of the triplet, or by combining the first two eighth notes of the triplet into a quarter. The result is like a triplet with a silent middle eighth note.

Once you get the hang of this "bouncy" feel, you'll never forget it...

Doug's Blues

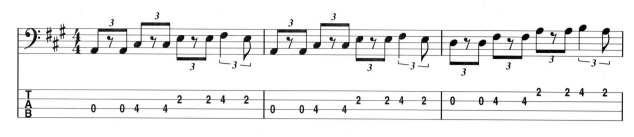

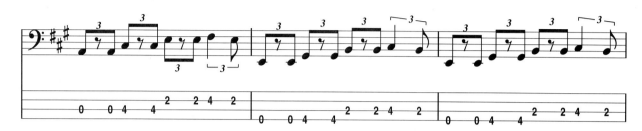

Shuffle notation can be hard to read. So instead, you'll often see straight eighth notes with the word "swing" or (♫ = ♩♪) written at the beginning of the song. This tells you to swing, or shuffle, all eighth notes.

Shuffle Head

► Pay close attention to the feel on this one.

Key Review

Track 49

When we see that the notes of a particular song come from a certain scale, we say that the song is *in the key* of that scale. For instance, if the notes of a song all come from the C major scale, we say that the song is in the key of C major.

Try playing the C major scale, but change the order of the notes. Begin and end your improvisation on the note C. Notice how the scale seems to be "at rest" when you arrive at C? This is because the note C is the root, or *tonic*—the note around which the key revolves.

Most major keys—except C major—contain sharped or flatted notes. Instead of writing these out as they occur, a *key signature* is used at the beginning of each line of music to tell you:

- What notes should be played sharp or flat throughout a song.
- The song's key (scale)

For example, the key of G major contains F♯, so its key signature will have a sharp on the F-line. This tells you to play all F notes as F♯ (unless, of course, you see a natural sign). This is what the scale would look like.

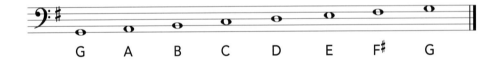

This table shows all the major keys and their corresponding flats or sharps.

Key	Number of Flats	Name of Flats	Key	Number of Sharps	Name of Sharps
C	0		C	0	
F	1	B♭	G	1	F♯
B♭	2	B♭, E♭	D	2	F♯, C♯
E♭	3	B♭, E♭, A♭	A	3	F♯, C♯, G♯
A♭	4	B♭, E♭, A♭, D♭	E	4	F♯, C♯, G♯, D♯
D♭	5	B♭, E♭, A♭, D♭, G♭	B	5	F♯, C♯, G♯, D♯, A♯
G♭	6	B♭, E♭, A♭, D♭, G♭, C♭	F♯	6	F♯, C♯, G♯, D♯, A♯, E♯

The Cycle of Fifths

You can also use the cycle of fifths to learn or memorize your key signatures. As you go clockwise around the circle, you move up by fifths. Interestingly, each new key along the circle has one more sharp (or one less flat) than the previous. Using our knowledge of intervals, moving up in fifths, helps us find our keys.

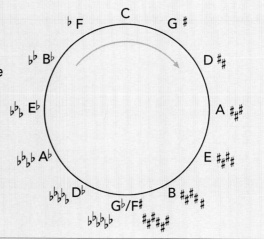

Let's practice reading in some major keys.

Track 50

Cruisin'

key of G

Track 51

Midnight

key of D

Try to figure out what key this is in by looking at the table of key signatures or the cycle of fifths.

Pottsie

Track 52

Transposition

Sometimes, you'll need to play a song in a different key than what it was originally written in—perhaps a key that's more comfortable for you, your band, your singer, etc. Changing the key of a song is called *transposition.* Try playing the following simple tune—"Yankee Doodle"—in the keys below. The transposition has already been done for you.

Track 53

Key of D

Key of C

Key of E

The Relative Minor

One easy way to learn minor keys is to relate them to their corresponding major key. It works like this: If you begin a major scale from its sixth degree, you'll find its *relative minor* scale. The relative minor, since it uses all the same notes as the major scale, also uses the exact same key signature.

For example, play a C major scale and count up to the sixth degree, A. Now play the scale starting from this note. This is the relative minor—the same notes, just played in different order, with a different emphasis. The order in which the notes are played results in a different sound.

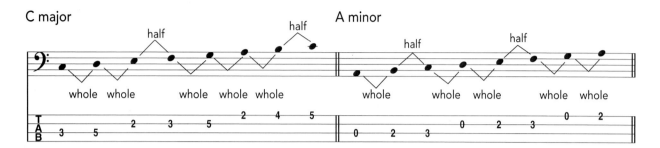

This table shows the major keys, their relative minors, and the number of flats or sharps.

Major Key	Relative Minor Key	Number of Flats	Major Key	Relative Minor Key	Number of Sharps
C	A minor	0	C	A minor	0
F	D minor	1	G	E minor	1
B♭	G minor	2	D	B minor	2
E♭	C minor	3	A	F# minor	3
A♭	F minor	4	E	C# minor	4
D♭	B♭ minor	5	B	G# minor	5
G♭	E♭ minor	6	F#	D# minor	6

Let's play some songs in minor keys.

Track 55

Minor Issue

This song is based in the key of E minor.

Track 56

Guilty

key of E minor

Track 57

Three Times

► This one's in D minor.

Ghost Notes

Ghost notes (sometimes called "dead notes") are percussive noises created by muting or deadening the string with the left hand while plucking with the right. They are notated using an "x" instead of a notehead.

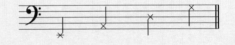

Can you guess the minor key being used here?

Track 58

Casper

Lesson 6 Chord Theory

Track 59

Understanding chords is an essential part of playing bass. This means knowing both what a chord is *and* what to play if you see a chord symbol in a piece of music. Chord symbols will be easy to master now that you've learned the major and minor scales and their intervals.

Remember: A *note* is one single pitch, an *interval* is two different pitches, and a *chord* is three or more different pitches sounded simultaneously.

Triad

A *triad* is the basic structure of most chords and is an important building block for bass lines. A triad consists of the root, third, and fifth of a scale. Let's take a look at a few major scales and find the triad within.

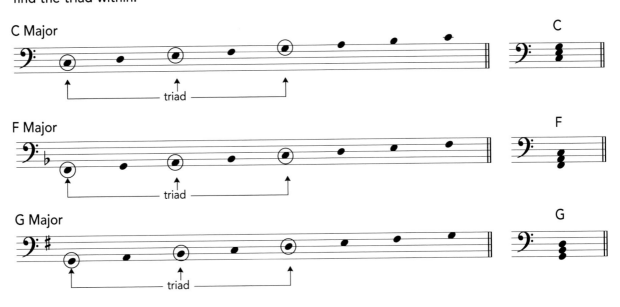

Now let's go over a few minor scales and find the triad within.

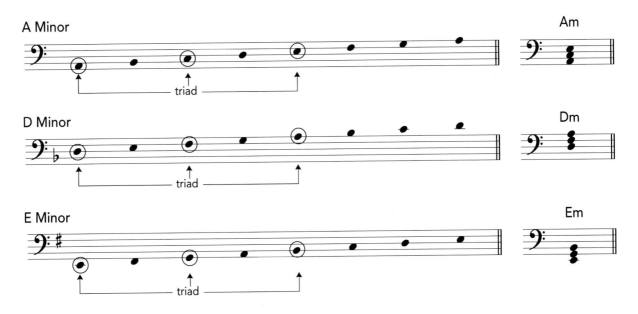

As a bassist, your job is to outline the chords—playing the notes one at a time—while other instruments such as piano or guitar play the actual chords above. Chords played one note at a time are called *arpeggios*. Let's play some arpeggios outlining major chords.

Chord symbols—such as "F" or "G"—are a form of musical shorthand, used in place of writing out the full chord name, like "F major" or "G major." When you see a single note name in a chart, it implies a major triad.

Track 60

Major Triads

► Start the G and C triads with the 2nd finger of your left hand.

Now we'll add the octave to our major triads.

Track 61

Major Triads & Octaves

Are you ready to move on to minor? Chord symbols for minor triads are labeled with an "m" after the note—for instance, Fm or Gm.

Track 62

Minor Triads

Now add the octave to our minor triads.

Track 63

Minor Triads & Octaves

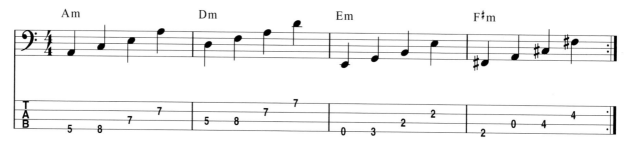

Let's combine our major and minor triads into progressions. The single element that is different between a major and minor triad is the third. A third, as you've already learned in our interval study, can be either major or minor.

Two, Five to One

To see how triads work in bass lines, we'll try a few songs.

Old Time

Slides

Slides are a type of articulation; they can add variety and interest to your bass lines. To play a slide like the ones shown, pluck the first note, and then sound the second note by sliding the same left-hand finger up or down along the string. (The second note is not picked.)

Sliding

Track 66

Bluesy Groove

Track 67

► This one's a stretch!

Adding The Seventh

The next step to understanding chord theory is adding the *seventh* to a chord. It's quite simple; when you see a chord labeled "maj7," it means the chord is built using the root, third, fifth, and seventh of a major scale.

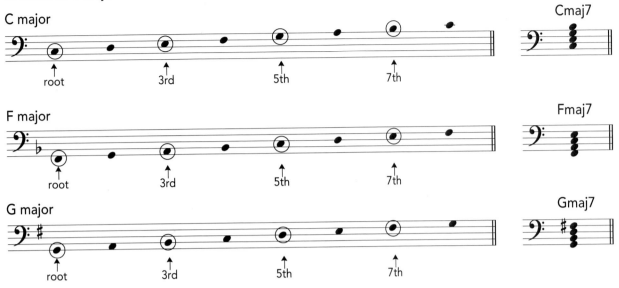

The same theory works for minor chords; when you see a chord labeled "m7," it means the chord is built using the root, third, fifth, and seventh of a minor scale.

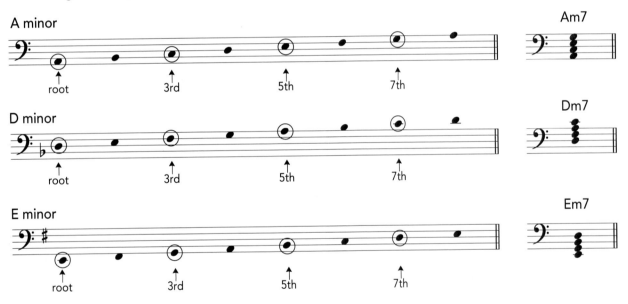

Let's play through some major seventh arpeggios, outlining the chords with the root, third, fifth, and seventh.

Major Sevenths

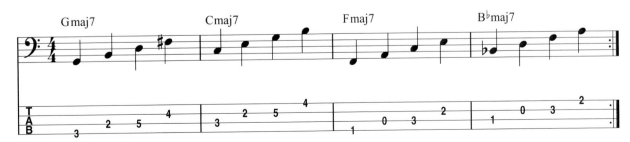

Now let's outline minor seventh chords.

Track 69

Minor Sevenths

When you're ready, let's combine major and minor seventh chords into some progressions. Keep in mind, the difference between these two chord types is the third and seventh intervals—in a major seventh chord, both intervals are major; in a minor seventh chord, both are minor.

Track 70

Seven & Seven

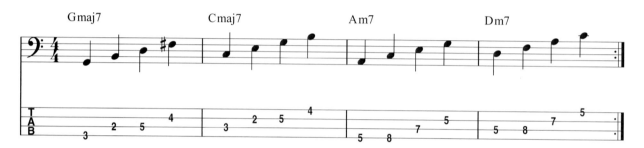

As a bassist, your job is to hold down the bottom end and to groove, so when playing over chords, you might not always play *every* note of a chord; for instance, sometimes you might play just the root. Nevertheless, understanding your options gives you creative choices and will add to the overall musicality of your bass lines.

Track 71

Busy Ballad

► Remember to read ahead!

1st and 2nd Endings

The next song has a *1st* and *2nd ending* (indicated by brackets and the numbers "1 and 2"). The first time through the song, play the 1st ending, up until the repeat sign, and then return to the beginning of the song. The second time through the song, skip the 1st ending and jump to the 2nd ending, playing until the end.

Track 72

Jamaican Beach

Chord Overview

Let's break down what we've learned about chords with a few simple formulas. These are shown in the key of C.

Chord Symbol	Scale	Intervals
C	Major	Root–M3–P5
Cm	Minor	Root–m3–P5
Cmaj7	Major	Root–M3–P5–M7
Cm7	Minor	Root–m3–P5–m7

The Dominant Scale

Track 73

One more scale to learn! This one is easy and very common. It's called the *dominant scale*; basically, it's the same as a major scale except that you flatten the seventh interval by a half step, making it a minor seventh. Let's take a closer look.

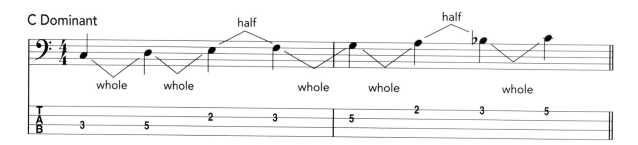

Notice the formula: whole–whole–half–whole–whole–half–whole.

Let's take a look at some more dominant scales.

Track 74

Dominant chords are famous for their unresolved sound and are used in all styles of music. Before we move onto a song, let's take a look at the dominant chord. It's built from the root, third, fifth, and seventh of a dominant scale. A dominant chord is labeled by putting a "7" after the root, such as C7 or G7.

C Dominant

C7 Arpeggio

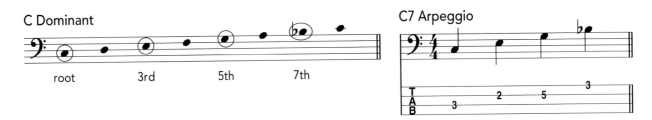

Track 75

Blue Dominant

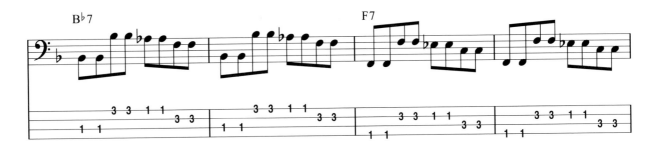

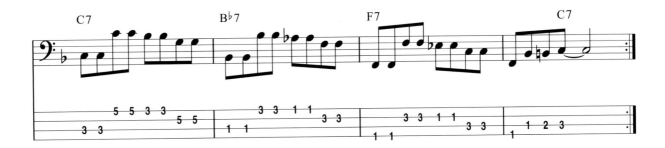

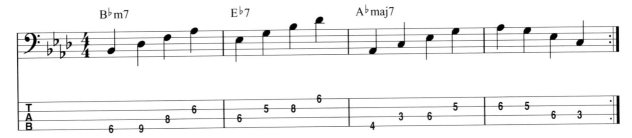

This song uses more than just dominant chords; listen to how the dominant chord (E♭7) wants to resolve.

Track 76

Jazzmine

12/8 Time

Reading in 12/8 time is a little tricky. There are 12 eighth notes in every measure, but they're typically grouped into four sets of three. This can feel like 4/4, but with three eighth notes per one beat, which gives it a swinging feel.

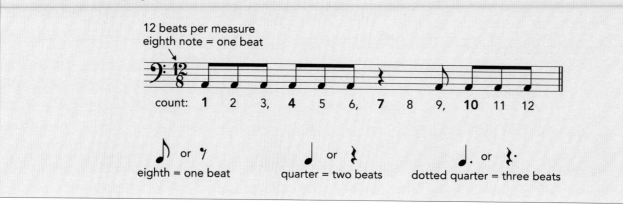

Let's try a 12/8 blues tune to help you get the feel for this new time signature.

Track 77

Chicago Shuffle

► Count aloud to keep the feel.

Another common time signature with this feel is *6/8*. To get a handle on this count, cut a 12/8 measure in half. 6/8 time usually has a much quicker feel than 12/8, so listen carefully before you try this one.

Track 78

Six Pack

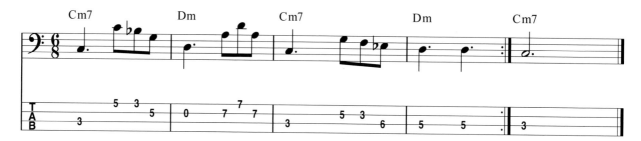

Slap Bass

Track 79

Slap bass is a style of playing widely used in funk, pop, soul, rock, and fusion music. It actually consists of two different techniques: the *slap*—using your thumb to slap (hit) the strings against the fingerboard; and the *pop*—using your index or middle finger to pull (snap) the string away from the fingerboard. Becoming fluent with these techniques requires a good deal of practice. Let's break them down!

Slap

This is the most important part of the technique; it's vital that you attain a good clean sound with your thumb before you move on to the pop. Attack or "slap" the string at the end of the fingerboard with the side of your thumb (at the joint), using motion from your wrist, not your arm. Let your thumb rebound (bounce) immediately (and rotate your wrist away) to allow the note to "ring" out. Bouncing the string against the fretboard and letting the string continue to vibrate creates the sound.

For starters, practice slapping half notes on the open stings. If the string is not ringing for the full two beats, practice bouncing off the string more quickly. The letter "T" (for "thumb") is used between staff and tab notation for this style.

Track 80

Thumb Open Strings

To get a good grasp on using your thumb, try your scales using the slap. For now, let's try another song!

Track 81

Digit

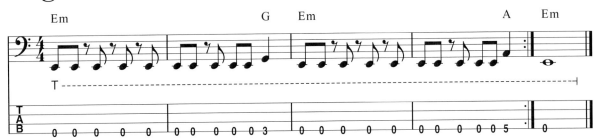

This song's a little longer, and it adds a few techniques from Level 1 to spice up the sound. Remember the pull-off and the hammer-on?

Drop the Hammer

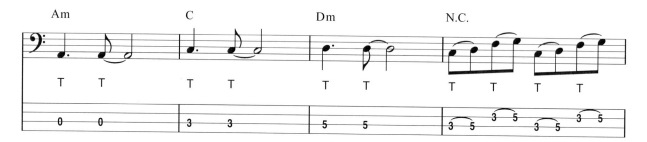

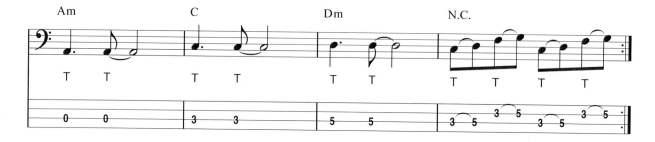

Pop

To pop a note, pull or "snap" the string away from the fretboard with your index or middle finger, again using your wrist for this motion. When released, the string will naturally rebound off the fretboard and "ring" out. Keep your right-hand fingers curled and in position to pop.

Ready to try the pop? The letter "P" is used between tab and staff notation to let you know that a note is popped.

Pop It

Let's combine the slap and pop using octaves.

Octagon

 Go slowly.

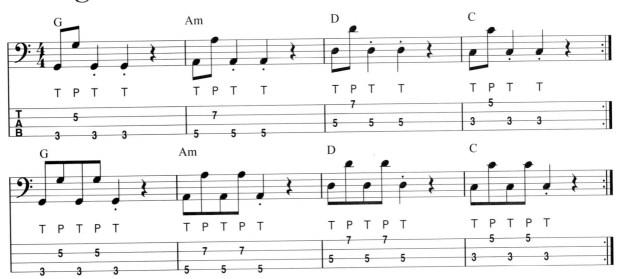

Wake Up

Practice your slap technique by applying it to songs you would normally play fingerstyle. It's a good idea not to do this in your band, but rather on your own time, getting fluid with your thumb. This style requires finesse, so take it slow and practice your notes cleanly and precisely.

We're adding one more thing to this example, the ghost note.

Track 86

Space Ghost!

► Ghost notes are very common in slap bass.

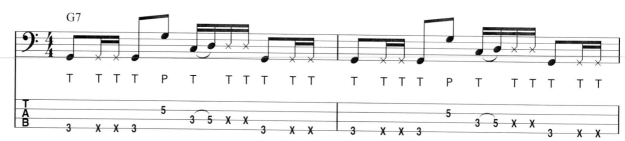

Rhythm Workout: The Thumb

Now let's review some rhythms and give your thumb a workout at the same time. As a bassist, your job is to have a great feel, and understanding rhythm gives you an advantage when it comes to grooving. So keep working at those rhythms!

A common figure is two sixteenth notes combined with an eighth rest; we'll start with both combinations of that rhythm so you get some practice. Use a thumb slap for each.

Track 87

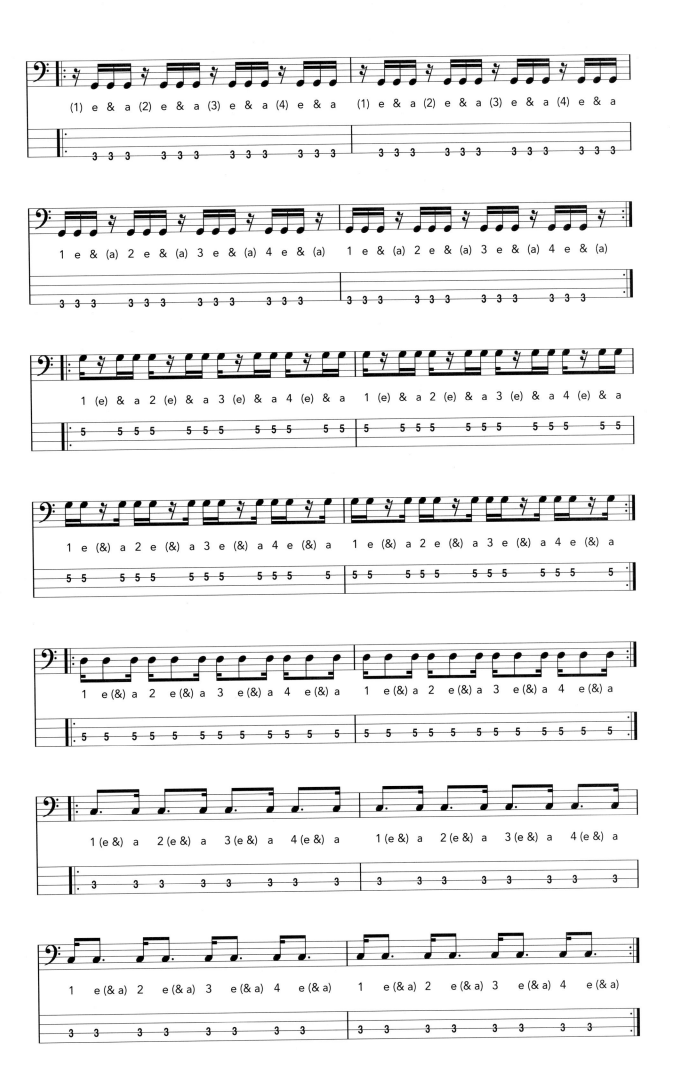

Locking In

Track 88

An important part of being a good bassist is being able to interact with a drummer. If you think about it, you are the connection between the rhythm and the harmony in your band. Your bass lines lock the grooves of the drums with the chords of the piano or guitar. That's a pretty big responsibility in the big picture of how a group sounds.

A great place to start working on your rhythm is listening to and "locking in" with the drummer. For the next examples, listen to the interaction between the bass and the bass drum.

Ballad

Pop Rock

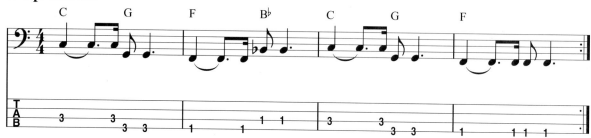

R&B

Funk

Now listen to how the bass plays along with the bass drum and *snare*. Many bass lines alternate to the fifth or octave of the chord as the drummer strikes the snare. We'll use the same grooves as track 88, so you can get an idea of what can be done.

Ballad

Pop Rock

R&B

Funk

Dynamics

Another way to help the groove is by accenting certain beats within a measure or within certain sections of a song. Changing *dynamics*—the degree of loudness or softness of your notes—helps to add more life to your bass lines. Dynamic markings are located beneath the staff, slightly before the note or notes affected. These are some of the most common:

pp	*pianissimo*	very soft
p	*piano*	soft
mp	*mezzo piano*	moderately soft
mf	*mezzo forte*	medium loud
f	*forte*	loud
ff	*fortissimo*	very loud
cresc.	*crescendo*	increasing loudness
decresc. or *dim.*	*decrescendo* or *diminuendo*	decreasing loudness
>	*accent mark*	play note louder

This is how these marks would look in a piece of music.

Dynamic Duo

Putting It All Together

Track 90

We're at the end—now it's time to put things together. With your knowledge of scales and chords, plus grooves and other odds 'n' ends, it's time to create your own bass lines in a practical situation.

Bass players are frequently required to read from chord symbols and to come up with bass lines on the spot. To be able to do that, one must understand chord structure and harmony, be familiar with how the bass functions in a variety of styles of music, and understand the role of a bassist, which is to create a supportive line for the melody.

Of course, every style is different; it takes time and a lot of listening to understand how the bass works in each specific idiom. For now, a sample bass line will be given to establish a basic groove, and you'll be expected to continue the same line, changing it to fit over the different chords.

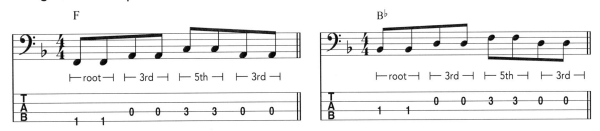

The first step is to analyze the bass line. Become familiar with it, look ahead to the chord changes, and transpose the line when needed.

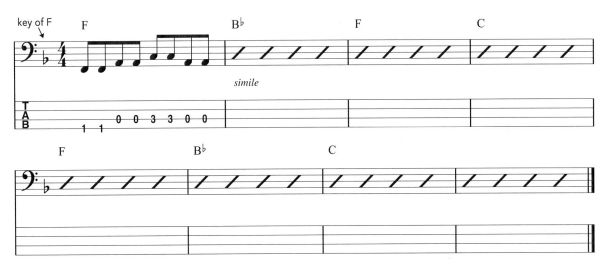

This could be what the bass line might look like when you're done.

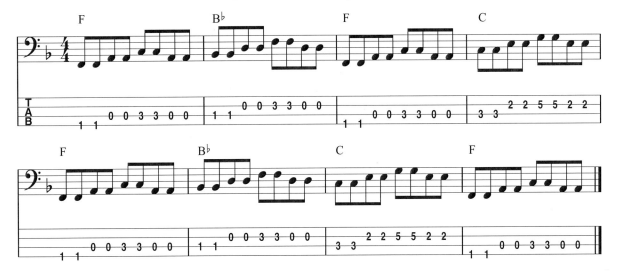

Let's start with a ballad. Watch the chord changes, and listen to the kick drum. The first four measures have the bass line written out for an example.

Now let's try the same song with a different bass line.

► Watch the chord changes, and work out the bass line before you start.

Ready for a blues? The first time, we'll play the bass line as a standard shuffle. The notes will be root, 3rd, 5th, and 3rd—all quarter notes—and we'll accent beats 2 and 4 to give it a better feel.

Track 93

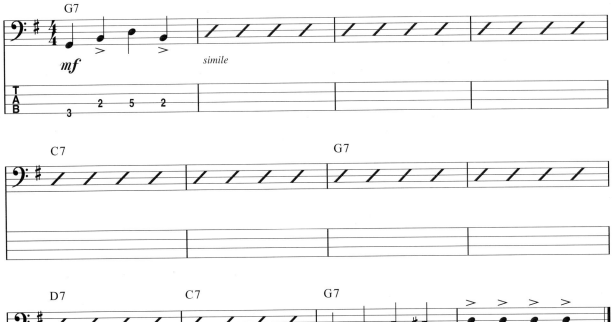

Let's get funky now! Pay attention to the groove on this one. The same chord changes as the last song, just a different feel.

Track 94

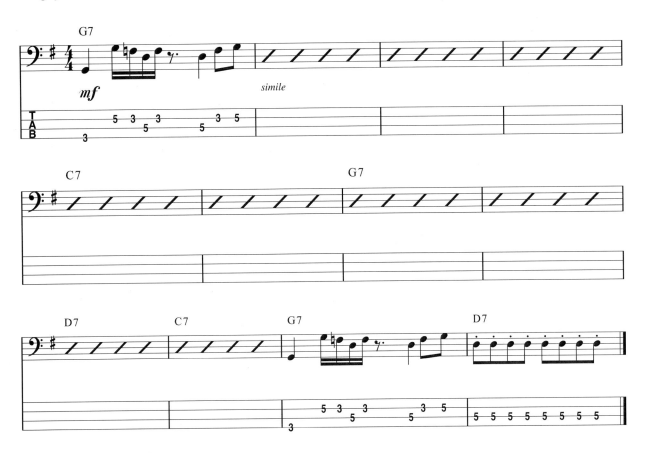

Rock, anyone? Stick to straight eighth notes the first time through. If you feel up to it, add the octave with the snare drum hits the second time.

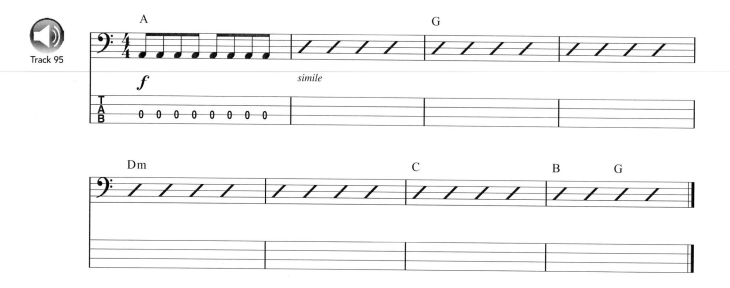

Same song, different groove. This bass line is a little more active.

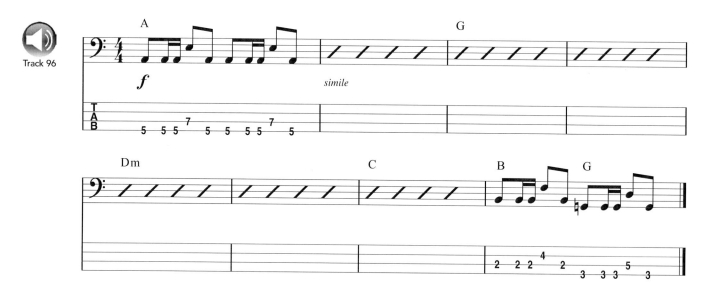

Slap style? Make sure you work out the bass line for this with all the chords ahead of time, just to be prepared.

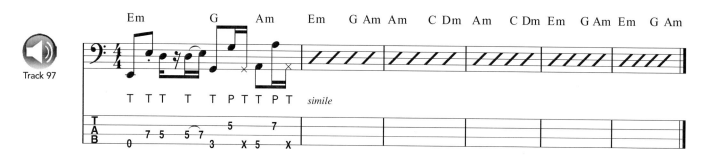

Try this song again, playing it fingerstyle without the slaps and pops—so you can appreciate the different sound that slap creates.

This song is a bossa nova. Watch the chord changes, and listen to how the bass fits in the pocket.

Track 98

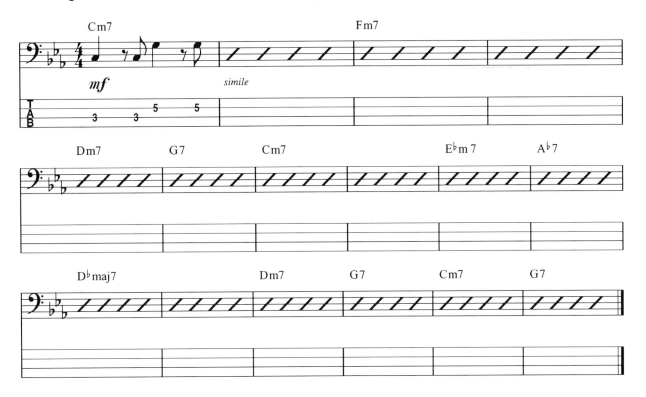

This one will be more difficult; we'll create a **walking bass** line. To "walk" a bass line, we outline the chord changes with quarter notes. There are many techniques for walking a bass line, but we'll keep it simple to start. For the first three quarter notes, play the triad of the chord, then on beat 4 use an **approach note**—a note one half step above or below the root of the chord you're approaching.

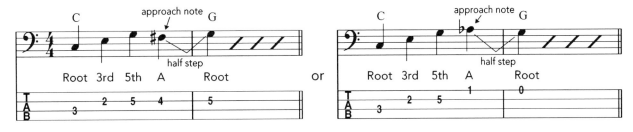

Ready? Here we go!

Track 99

Review

Notes on the Fretboard

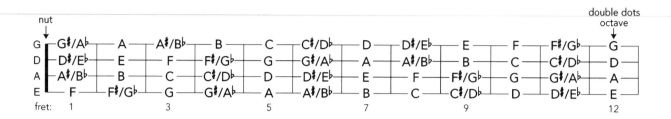

Notes in Fifth Position

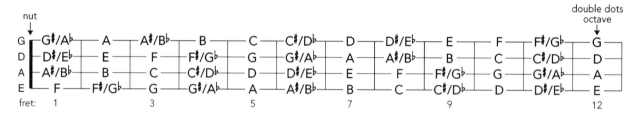

Major, Minor, and Dominant Scales and Chords

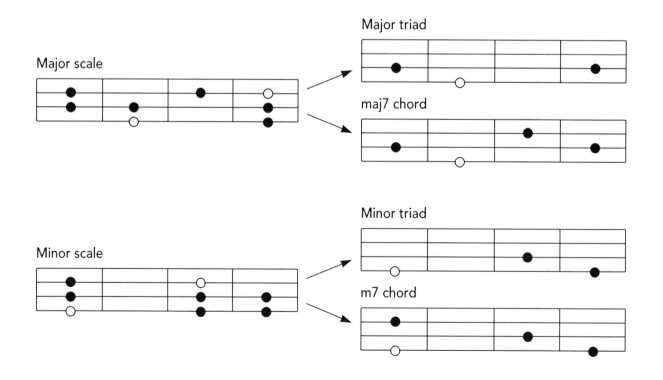

Major scale

Major triad

maj7 chord

Minor scale

Minor triad

m7 chord